THE GHOST IN THE GEARS

THE GHOST IN THE GEARS

Howard White

HARBOUR PUBLISHING

Published by
HARBOUR PUBLISHING
P.O. Box 219
Madeira Park, BC Canada V0N 2H0

Cover design by Roger Handling
Cover illustration by Gordon Labredt
Printed and bound in Canada

CANADIAN CATALOGUING IN PUBLICATION DATA

White, Howard, 1945 --
    Ghost in the gears

    Poems.
ISBN 1-55017-065-1

    I. Title.
PS8595.H57G5 1993   C811'.54   C92-091162-5
PR9199.3.W54G5 1993

ACKNOWLEDGEMENTS

Poems in this book have appeared previously in the following places:

Event
Working
Raven
Ruebsaat's
New Catalyst
BC *Bookworld*
CBC Radio *Morningside*
CBC Radio *Gabereau*
Writing in the Rain
Paperwork (Tom Wayman)
Going for Coffee (Tom Wayman)

As usual it took a completely ridiculous amount of handholding and nosewiping to coax this manuscript into existence and my heartfelt thanks go out to Steve Osborne; Alan Twigg; to the great encourager, Tom Wayman; and to my unfailing partner, publisher and muse, Mary Lee White.

This book is dedicated to Silas and Patrick.

CONTENTS

INTRODUCTION

Not so long ago an old school friend who got on steady at the local college was good enough to invite me over to her class to read some of my poems out loud. After I'd read everything I'd written in the last ten years, which took us up to the first smoke break, one of the students put her hand up and said, "That was rilly good in some places, Mr. White, but how can you tell what you write is poetry and not prose?"

Damn. I could remember the discussions of what makes poetry poetry being carried on with some heat in my own school days, replete with belligerent factions armed with slogans:

"Poetry is language charged with meaning to the utmost possible degree."

"Poetry is news that stays news."

"No ideas but in things."

"Two legs good, four legs bad . . ."

Even with the omniscience of youth I had trouble picking who was right, and the relentless mass murder of braincells which had taken place in the intervening years didn't make my position any easier. Still, I felt I owed it to the reputation of Living Authors to attempt some sort of reply.

"Prose doesn't have rhyming words at the ends of the lines."

"But neither does your, ah, writing."

She had me there. I had no choice but to escalate the discussion into a consideration of poetic measure and how it can be discerned in a given composition. First you must carefully examine the text in order to ascertain where the poem in question begins and where it ends. Then you measure the entire distance between those two points using a good quality ruler. If it's over 18 inches (40 cm) long, the thing is most likely to be prose. If it's under that you can take chance on it being poetry—unless it's obviously a grocery list.

On second thought—I can't be too sure about grocery lists. I am seeing more of these being accepted as poems lately. If all else failed one could try checking the cover of the book. Even in these morally bankrupt times there are few books containing poetry which do not carry a plain warning on the front cover, although even here, one of our more distinguished practitioners has been known to disguise his art in books which appear to be about more accepted subjects such as protective footwear.

It was meeting the Palestinian poet Fawaz Turki that relieved me of a lot of the anxiety it seems normal to have about whether the stuff you're filling your book up with is poetry or something else just as short. I met Fawaz at a big Amnesty International jamboree of oppressed writers in Toronto a few years ago, and one of the things that intrigued me about him was a rumour that he might be reduced to chopped liver by a Mossad hit squad at any time. I found it invigorating to think that I was sharing the planet with people who cared enough about poetry to massacre anybody over it, and I went to readings by Fawaz and a number of persecuted poets from other third-world nations, hoping to discover what they were doing to earn such respect. Their poetry was the plainest stuff you could imagine:

> I hate nobody
> I rob nobody
> but when I starve
> I eat the flesh of my marauders
> Beware . . . my hunger

A lot of it had been written for special occasions, the signing of a treaty, the loss of another leader, a meeting to warn mothers against Nestle milk nurses etc. and I was astonished by the bold way they used the poem as a tool of public communication—flexible, effective, unpretentious, but with a certain disposable quality that didn't come across very well at a high-toned literary event in downtown Toronto. Fawaz started with a good audience, but it was half gone by the time he finished. The CanLit crowd was prepared to overlook a little terrorism but they drew the line at news that didn't stay news. I was embarrassed on my country's behalf and decided to invest a beer in some international fence-mending.

I needn't have worried. Fawaz was used to western writers finding third world poetry too prosy and journalistic but he had more than enough ego reinforcement from his own people to feel secure about what he was doing. Back in Jordan, he told me, it was nothing to have a crowd of several thousand gather on a few hours notice to hear him at an open-air reading. When he appeared in public, throngs of grown women followed him around ululating and fluttering their hands like leaves, chanting his name. His broadsheets outsold newspapers. And he wasn't alone. There were Palestinian poets more popular than him, and there were many Eastern Bloc and Latin American poets whose books sold huge quantities in underground editions. I'd heard of these incredibly popular South American poets before—Earle Birney has a poem about it—but I'd never considered it much more than a wondrous curiosity. It was quite a novelty to think the very idea poetry is a dying art form might be a western conceit which doesn't apply to vast portions of the globe.

At a bull session later some CanLit prof asked why poetry was less marginalized in so many developing countries and about 17 third-worlders tried to answer at once. The general drift was, western poets have done it to themselves because all they do is write for each other. They consider it corruption of true art to write for common taste, but they're never done whining that the public fails to appreciate them. And even when poets from developing countries show how well the public responds to poets who write for common taste with serious purpose, western writers fail to get the message. Somebody tried to make a case that western writers didn't have the kind of big social challenges poets in developing worlds did, but gave up when somebody else yelled, "Try taking your culture back from Hollywood and Madison Avenue!"

It would be nice if I could tie this ramble together by saying this third-world poetic ricocheted across the hemisphere to galvanize my attempts to fashion poetry from bush life in Pender Harbour BC, but the fact is I'd already spent years fiddling at the kind of prosy weather reports to be found herein. What it did was give me a little relief from those nagging questions about what makes poetry poetry. Whatever it is, these are some of the words that were useful to me, at various times. I'm struck with the inappropriateness of placing many of these pieces in anything so static and exclusive as this pricey litle book—for most of them I would have preferred a spot on the local breakfast broadcast or editorial page where they might have provided a chuckle or a moment of reflection and been disposed of. In our world, those are the spaces most in need of what poetry has to offer, the frontier where the battle for cultural survival must be renewed, and my best hope for this motley collection is that it contains a few steps toward the kind of poem that could do that work.

The Ghost in the Gears

Finally starting to get in the swing of this job
after a morning of false starts, near misses and spills
men starting to stand closer to the bucket of my backhoe
trusting me better than I do myself
the machine moves up the slope, slips the load between
    them,
swoops back in a neat controlled glide, nudges a drum
two guys struggle to move, not knowing they needed my
    help
they smile, one says, "Okay! Now we're cookin!"
The machine moves around me without the intervention
    of thought
my hands flowing over the levers like an expert typist until
I reach for the wrong one
the machine lurches
                  men leap
for their lives
as the one-ton boulder teeters, almost falls
where they were standing, settles safely back.
What the hell? But I know what it was. I reached for swing
and got stabilizer instead, not simply forgetting but
remembering where that lever was on some machine from
    the past.

It happens about once a year, disrupting my unconscious
    motion,
a palpable ghost I strain to identify—
it couldn't be the old rattletrap Case I worked on last
Its broken seat and sharp, neurotic swing motion
that never could be trusted to become instinctive

are too fresh and I'm too conscious of unlearning it.
This was one from earlier, that snuck up on unsuspecting
      instinct
I go over all the backhoes I have been familiar with
like an aging Casanova counting his women —
not so many in fact, I've been more faithful than they
      deserved

There was the JCB up at Port Hardy, a gutless old girl
with exceptional balance, or Sparrow's John Deere
that had terrific reach but kept breaking its boom
all of those had pedal swings just like this new 580-D —
couldn't be any of them.
                    That old Sherman I learned on
had lever swings, one on each side
with rubber grips forever coming off
a tiny machine with hoses sticking out everywhere,
you'd be snagging one every move
getting showered with overheated oil and once
hammering away on a hardpan grave
my swamper Hawkeye Charlie alongside
leaning on his muckstick half asleep
one of those hoses rubbed on a battery post
until the rubber rubbed through
exposing the wire core
which shorted out
releasing a shower of sparks and boiling oil
transforming my dinky little backhoe
into an military-strength flamethrower
swamping Charlie in a swirling ball of black-orange flame

it was Christmas before his eyebrows grew back
you never knew what would happen next
but we built half the town with that machine
coming back like thirty years hadn't passed
something kind of nice about that

The men crawl back to their places, standing just as close
as before
grins on their faces
showing

they all believe in ghosts

Tiresias II

That must be really interesting, doing the garbage dump
they say. I try to think how.
They tell me I ought to find interesting stuff.
They ask me if I can read the garbage like Christie Logan
Seem to expect me to make prophecies about our
     civilization
I think over the stuff I see up there.
For a catskinner used to ploughing
the clean and trackless wastes of the north
it is interesting to find Tampax
jammed into the track-adjuster hole
panty-hose wound around the sprockets
bank records impacted into the belly-pan
it is interesting to realize a healthy HD7-G
can stall dead out trying to move a heap
of used pampers the size of the Community Hall
it is interesting that most people don't seem to care
what the dump guy knows about the bad condition
of their underwear or Mastercharge account
while others compulsively set fire
to everything even their dogfood cans
causing the whole dump to flare up
in an apocalyptic pillar of orange and green and black
that towers over the town like a mushroom cloud
filling the local paper with irate letters
and causing me to hauled on the carpet to face dumb
dump questions I can't answer
because breathing the virulent fumes
has reduced my voice to a reedy squeak for over a week

It is interesting when the whole five-acre lump
begins to glow like plutonium
and the town's weekly crop of screwtop wine jugs
begins to explode with dull artillery thuds
ripping up through the ground like Titan missiles
and a forty-pounder of Sommet Rouge smokes past my ear
to splash against the grid behind my unprotected head
giving me brief intimations of mortality —
maybe that's the sort of thing they're looking for.
I have kept my eye open for dead babies
blackened in the sun, finding none
but once there were three bloated sheep, shot in the heads
someone's back-to-the-land project over with a vengeance
and for prophecy it did occur as the pampers
balled up before me the size of a barn
there could be another population explosion on the way.
This was a year before the sociologists
came out with the same news on TV.

But don't you get some sort of vision of society's underbelly?
You're an archaeologist of the present
can't you describe us by our leavings?

I tell them about the lack of anything old
everything people throw out was new last year
broken-backed sofas the size of a compact car
tinsely fabric still gleaming in the sooty firelight
plush carpet smelling of dog
more fridges and automatic washers and
electric hot water tanks than stones in a field

masses of plastic
kindergarten lunchbuckets decorated with last year's TV hit
kitchen gismos briefly made indispensable by a K-Tel ad
toy bulldozers designed by someone who clearly never saw
    one
all the inventive genius of our century come to rest
in a single anonymous heap of red yellow blue
it is a long, depressing list that adds up, in the end,
to very little
my admirers tend to frown and change the topic
but then us prophets are used to that

Loonshit

You couldn't tell to look at it it would be mud
at least I couldn't, not then, my catskinner's eye
for what lies beneath the world's unsuspecting feet
still untrained
it looked like a solid grassy slope
and it was solid the first few passes —
Clear the brush off and level it up, Fred said and left us to it.
It wasn't until I hooked a stump and spun the tracks a bit
the big Eight fell through and wallowed up to its fenders
in loonshit.
I was lucky to crawl back out onto solid ground.
I tried different places along the slope but it was all the
    same —
once you broke through the crust the machine flopped
    helpless
in muck, the power of its 600 strong draught horses
reduced to that of a sickly pup.
By noon I had the whole area gouged up
in a swarming mass of gullies and hadn't cleared a stick,
desperate to find a way to beat the muck
before the boss came back but the more I tried the worse it
    got
I tried backing onto solid ground and running at it hard
I tried sneaking around the edges
I tried coming up from the bottom and coasting back
but once that 50-ton bulldozer touched the mud
it lost all reason for being
wallowing useless making things worse.
I gave up trying to do the job and started
just trying to smooth over the mess I'd made

skimming backwards along the slope
until I got so stuck I had to climb off the machine
and spend an hour mud-wrestling boulders and chunks to
    claw free
leaving a serpentine river of slop across the job
just in time to be seen by Fred
who took in my day of distress at a glance and said
Can't you get under that mud?
It's bottomless, I said.
There's nothing you can do with it.
But Fred was already up on the cat
diving straight into the gumbo
wallowing, yawing, driving down deeper than I dared to go
till suddenly the cat gave a hard jerk
took hold, levelled itself off deep in a trough
and began to regain its purpose in creation,
thrusting solidly forward as waves of ooze rolled away on
    each side.
Behind I could see a trail of dry red shale emerging.
Fred took one pass and climbed off.
That stuff's only four feet deep. You just gotta go below it to
    where you can get some traction.
I had decided the whole earth had gone to slop, down to
    the core.
That there was solid ground so close at hand seemed
    incredible
but knowing that key fact
I had no trouble putting the mud on the run in short
    order.

I've never got bogged down since
whether in mud, red tape or red ink
without thinking
I wonder how deep the loonshit is this time?

Sidetrip

After Jim Spilsbury

We started quite slowly, thinking to run out of track
every few yards, but eventually we got our nerve up
and were clipping along about 30 mph
beetling down the length of this unnamed valley
passing through gullies and over trestles by the dozen.
We could see around quite well, as the whole country
was logged off to the last stick,
leaving an endless plain of stumps and brush
grown up four feet high in fireweed and thistles
which set up a terrific cloud of down and leaves behind
    the speeder
as we passed a small lake about half a mile in length
and several dry lake bottoms grown over with thick grass
through which were trails, probably bear.
Next we cut through a depression and into another valley,
followed up the side of this for about a mile or so
and then made a U-turn and came back along the other
    side,
gradually climbing to an altitude of about 1000 feet.
Neither of us had any idea which way we were travelling.
After hours of this we came to abandoned equipment
including three donkeys and several cars on sidings,
and a cluster of bunkhouses like a deserted village.
Everything had been left as they were using it
utensils in the kitchen, the oil in the lamps,
the cookhouse with sixteen tables set for twelve men each.
By the calendars left on the bunkhouse walls
and two-foot high alders between the ties
I reckoned it must have been abandoned about three years.
I asked the speederman how much further the track went

but he had no idea.
We quit at this point as we didn't want to run out of gas.
I spent the next few weeks asking anybody I could find
about the country we'd seen, trying to determine
just how much further we could have gone,
but no one knew, and few showed any interest.
I couldn't get over it.
In all there were 35 donkeys and 12 steam locomotives
scattered around in those woods,
the remains of a lumbering empire gone to waste.
It was like a lost world out there,
a vast ruin as big as a European country,
which had been created so casually it had no name.
I couldn't stop trying to picture those loggers,
logging out their lives in those nameless valleys
forgotten by the time the alder was two foot high.
You couldn't help wondering about the meaning of it.
What had driven them to create this barrens so great
it was probably big enough to be seen from the moon?
Money? But the whole enterprise had ended in bankruptcy.
What did that mean?
Whatever it meant, it was giving no pause
to the new wave of loggers busily setting up
among the ruins, eager to swipe the last
great fir forest off the face of the earth.
Nor to me,
just as eagerly providing their need for communication.
We were caught in something,
something we did as much in spite of
the end result as for it.
There were moments like this when I glimpsed through it,

saw the whole industrial process resolving itself
in a meaningless pattern, but then the picture wavered
and I was back in pitching with the best of them.

Scabby Mackay

Poor old Scab, he opposed that one strike in '37,
joined the union later and paid his dues
but 40 years later they still shunned him
at the Minstrel Island pub
forcing him to claw his lonely arthritic way
up the slippery slope of a one-man salvage claim
he kept up more for the sake of appearances
than to make any money, subsidizing the gas bill
with his old-age pension cheque
just so he wouldn't have to admit
the scissorbills had finally beat him.
He'd stop all along his long climb to work
plant little patches of tomato and pansies
along the skid path, talk to the old mama bear
bullshit endlessly with any unsuspecting tourist —
he could talk into coming along, like us —

Old Scab, he didn't get one busted chunk in the water
every other day and what he did boom up
the bugs ate long before he found a buyer
but he never stopped railing about
how the big cumpney's were rooning the province
naming the sins of all the long succession
of Liberal and Social Credit cabinet ministers —
he quoted you chapter and verse of all the
offending bills and acts and nefarious rules
by which the logger's once-proud calling was undone
but his complaint went on: the Davis plan,
which had ruined the fishing industry
and David Lewis's cozying up to the Trudeau Liberals

were all acts of near treason he couldn't
contemplate without being seized with rage

Sitting in his little stove-oil-soaked floatshack
he not too apologetically called
"The black hole of Calcutta"
swilling greasy coffee and scratching fleas
he summed it all up: Canadians, he said,
were the stupidest people in the world.
He liked the way that came out: Yes, he said,
and said it again: *We Canadians, we gotta be the
stupidest damn race of people that ever walked.*
I can't say as how I was too convinced
by this rather sweeping generality
but since then, oh, how many times,
watching Davis get convicted of fraud
yet enjoy re-election time after time
watching the rape of the forests and rivers
not only go on as before, but escalate enormously
at the hands of forest conglomerates
now more than ever owned by foreign profiteers
watching the Tories throw in our energy and water
as a little signing bonus to the free trade deal —
how many times have I thought of old Scab
hunched on the doorstep of his floating hovel
shouting those fateful words across
the dark saltchuck of memory:

We Canucks are the goddamn stupidest people in the world!

The Oldtimer Talks Economics

The oldtimer says
capitalism is like witchcraft
it teaches us we can't do anything
without money
same as the witchdoctor told the Indians
you can't do anything
without spirits
they say now Canada can't have her own Merchant Marine
we have the ports we have the shipyards
we have the steel we have the sailors
we have the freight
we have the world's longest waterfront
we could do it all ourselves
but they say we haven't got the money
and we believe them
so we don't do it

During the depression
they said we didn't have the money
to feed the nation's babies
and we believed them
we let the babies twist up with rickets
then war came and overnight we built
a merchant navy of 1000 ships —
we were so scared we forgot about money
and did it without
made Canada the fourth largest shipowning nation.
Soon as the war was over the dollar-a-year men
broke the fleet up, pretended it never happened
got us all back to our old belief

you can't build a ship unless
you go on bended knee to New York
same as the Indian can't catch a whale
unless he goes on bended knee to the witchdoctor
so the witchdoctor gets half the whale
same as Rockefeller gets half the ship

then Mao comes along, covers China in dams and
factories, delivers 600 million from starvation
without borrowing a cent from Rockefeller
and the capitalists denounce him
with all the fervour of a witchdoctor
denouncing science
because they're both the same
the shaman's mumbo-jumbo
the capitalist money-myth
just two kinds of mind control

Invisible Minority

There are 1 million Canadian unemployed.
That's enough to stretch from Vancouver
to Calgary if placed head to foot
on their bellies along the Trans Canada Highway.
If placed in CPR cattlecars, they
would make a train 57 miles long.
If shot by firing squads, they would require
a pyramid of bullets 300 feet high
and a mass grave the size of the *Globtik Tokyo*.
If ground up and reduced to meat paste,
they would make a string of sausages
reaching from sea to shining sea

and if reduced to a percentage decrease
of point oh-seven points over the previous quarter
they can be made to vanish entirely

The Executive

The executive had risen to the top
sitting long hours at his desk on the 41st floor
drinking rare blends of coffee
made for him by his gorgeous aide
He used to drink urn coffee
from the cafeteria but grew bored
and began using the company's overseas agents
to bring in the rarest blends known
this was no indulgence he knew now
this was his duty as president
of a firm richer than the whole
Austro-Hungarian Empire
the work itself was no longer demanding
even though he was known
as a working president
with his fingers in everything
it was easier to have your fingers in things
than to do them
and it was no hard thing
to tell a manager to excel
the trick was to make him think
you'd told him something special
to create a mystique
to be inscrutably elite
to always find some brilliant new way
of saying "buy low, sell high"
to avoid obvious blunders.
There were decisions, certainly
new territories to be opened
new victims begging for takeover
like objects in a child's game of marbles

no harder to hit for being bigger
his born indifference to scale
and his mastery of the manner of power
his true qualification for the job.
The worst position he'd ever had
was at the start, in publishing
where he'd had to do everything himself.
Doing jobs was hard, much harder
than ordering them done.
He had been no good at doing things,
himself, and it had troubled him.
He thought someday he would understand
how things got done
but here he sat with a workforce
the size of Napoleon's army
supporting the economies of one Canadian province
and several small dictatorships in the third world
and all he could do was pray
the great machine kept finding its way
but it was not something a wise president
could afford to think about —
if it faltered the company
would get a new president
and he would get a new company

Has Anyone Seen the Working Class?

For Tom Wayman

I.

A young American woman with a PhD has written me
saying she wants to devote her life to the working class
and can't decide if it should be in some third-world country
or Canada. I haven't been able to reply for over a year
although I feel an uncertain responsibility
to speak up for our bunch

A friend I owe much to has put her up to this
after reading some things I wrote about driving cat
and I struggle to be worthy
of their confidence: *the working class*
the *Canadian* working class — oh thou elusive wraith,
long have I avoided this moment of truth

I think of my cousin who still gets dirty for money
— but pulls down more in a year than the local doctor

I think of the late Communist Party and its confident talk
of a Canadian proletariat — but then at election time
polling fewer votes than the Rhinoceros Party

I think of the time that student marxist group at UBC
got all charged up with its own propaganda
and marched down to free the embattled workers at
        Canron
and the Canron bosses had to call the riot squad in
to stop the men from leaving their work
to pound the piss out of these damnfool students

I think of all those loggers I grew up with
how they would turn away from any attempt
to class them together, especially
as any sort of underprivileged species
— the funny look that would pass between them
when some hapless tourist came to camp
and made the mistake of saying "you fellows . . ."
in that special class self-conscious way . . .

I think of how the young guys wanted so much to be rich,
to go to Hawaii and drive a new Cadillac
instead of a ten-year-old one
as long as this wouldn't make them into shits

I think of how some did get rich
and liked it fine
although they didn't do so good
at not becoming shits

I think of how the the gillnet fishermen
used to mock their ever-so-serious union rep
and how they didn't care to hear
that what they thought was a proud career
was just some smarter men making monkeys of them
I think of how the one word I never heard
in the workingclass town where I grew up
was the word workingclass

II.
The more I think about it the more the Canadian working
    class
takes on the shape of some impossible fiction

until this one Saturday in January Sticks Andersen
a salt-soaked old troller who's been around forever
is sitting in my kitchen bitching about the price of
    live-landed lingcod
and another neighbour, a nice-enough guy from the city
who has never worked with his hands and has a bigger
    house
for weekends than we do for all year round
comes tapping at the door to see if we can help him
start this little bitty powersaw he got for Christmas.
He's got the operator's manual memorized
but cranks it like a baby — one good snap is all it takes
and he's tickled as hell — "I was afraid I had a lemon," he
    says

We can see he'll never get the load of firewood
he wants for his new Swiss parlour heater
he'll saw both feet off first
but Sticks doesn't want to make him feel bad
so he says, "By God, I could use some wood myself . . ."
and we lead the guy back in the bush with our own
    battered Stihls

"What size wood does that there new boiler of yours take?"
Sticks asks and we rip through a bunch of nice downed fir

as our friend frets and fusses with his saw
measuring off each cut with a steel tape —

"We musn't mix up our pieces," he cautions us with
    irritation
tugging his few hard-clawed chunks away from the growing
    pile

"Well, you know, this is comin pretty easy here," Sticks
    says,
"Why don't you just pull your bus up here and we'll
    throw on a load."
"But most of this is *yours* . . ." the guy stammers,
realizing for the first time we've cut every piece to his size,
"I couldn't let you . . . you must take some for yourselves . . ."
"Ah, me 'n Flash here can get wood any time,"
Sticks replies. "We'll come back tomorrow."
"This is worth money . . ." the other mumbles,
digging out keys to his new Cherokee Chief and breaking
    into a trot

leaving Sticks and I standing there confronted
once again
by all the difference that is class

Street Crazies

I wouldn't want it said I have enjoyed the
worst of misfortunes that can befall
a fellow human, namely loss of mind
but I must in honesty confess
a helpless lifelong fascination
for lunatics who haunt the streets

It is only in the heart of the city
that you see them. Never in suburbs.
Never in sidestreets or byways.
For them nothing but the prime traffic areas
of the continent: Times Square,
Georgia and Granville, Sherbrooke
and The Main — Montreal with its pride
in civilized culture adorns itself
with trilingual crazies who shrug their way
along the art-strewn esplanades
conducting brilliant five-part Platonic dialogues
with themselves. New York, with the best
of everything has real lepers
with dangling eyeballs and bloody stumps
to thrust out at the minkhatted theatregoers
who don't bat an eye

One mute crone wears out the gentrified
paving stones of downtown Vancouver
perhaps in rain but noticed only in shine
carrying an open umbrella
having sacrificed everything
for this one last trenchant comment

on the city's unforgiveable weather
saying it for all of us

Today, marvelling as I pass
along South Granville
wondering what is to be made of this bizarre mix
of rank pornography and cheap electronic gimmicry
seizing, like some symbiotic space-age plague
at the heart of our age

I see a derelict with matted beard
and red, burning eyes
raving his mad answer
into a broken walkie-talkie
which he folds up, turns off
and replaces in his greatcoat pocket
stopping a few paces further on
to remove it again
extend the bent antenna
and holding it close to his scabby lips
unleash another soaring ecstatic tirade
into its lifeless diodes

tragic, mad — no doubt:
but I can't shake the conviction
these tortured messages contain
intelligence of more crucial import
than anything on the working channels
if only we knew
how to receive them

Culture

The Indians used to tell stories to their kids
about Raven and Mink
bringing disaster through
resource mismanagement

kept their whole show sustainable
bound it together flesh and bone
with this tissue of instruction

Today while our leaders
charge up $400 billion for
just what we don't rightly know
and foreigners lay the forest to waste
our children watch GI Joe

Poem Ending with a Line by Raymond Carver

An acquaintance of mine, a man who
works assiduously for a US giant
manufacturer of food additives, atomic reactors,
feminine supplies and oil pipelines
and is quietly resigned
to the moral dilemmas of our age
tells me the oil industry is quaking
in their boots over a
bacterium
that inhabits the swift-flowing
corridors of the world's great
oil pipelines, massing dangerously
in any slight bend
eating the steel away to nothing

our computer repairman tells me
what Silicon Valley hasn't figured out
is a solution to the bacterium
that lives on the contacts
of our computer's memory chips
gorging themselves on white-collar electrons
until their unshakeable insistence
on living
forces the connection apart
and the nation's business stops
those bacteria

are the heroes of this poem

From Book Blurbs to the Bomb

Back a few years ago I remember
my first book blurb
for an ad in a magazine

I slaved for days, harassed beyond sense
by the crushing responsibility
of placing these words before the waiting world
saying all that needed to be said
to jar the indifferent millions to attention
while doing honest justice
to the book's sacred purpose
at the same time, producing copy
crabbed and too clever by half

Now I toss blurbs off in a minute
or borrow them whole from the intro
thinking, "Not great but it'll pass"
move the job along
knowing the world is not waiting
and won't accept genius as an excuse
for missed deadlines

Knowing the great corporations
get by with even less
not having poets to write their copy

This world isn't what it seems
to the man on the street —
with a wave of the hand
a general throws a battalion into Dieppe

thinking better of it
amid reports of terrible slaughter
at tea the next day

and Reagan wobbly with late-night whisky
fingers the red button
trying to decide what a
first-rate star like Bogie or Duke
would do in his place

history scribbling itself down

Timewarp

When we first moved to this property
we would put on hiking boots and pack a snack
to go through the trees and brush to our back line.
We seemed to own a good chunk of the BC wilderness.
Now that we've cleared it the kids run it in a minute
and we wonder what happened to all that space.
So with time. Using *page down* I flip through
a chapter that took me two months to write,
deleting the signs of strain and references
to vast periods of time passing by
in a piece that takes only minutes to read.
My mind goes back to those pioneers
who came to this country after year-long ordeals
in steerage, battling storms around the Horn,
ambushes and broken wheels across the plains,
but fell down kissing the earth when they arrived
where now I hop a jet and pass over in the time
it takes to complete my fourth viewing of *Tootsie*,
the prize made poor by ease of winning.
Old Hubert Evans was on nights at the *Mail & Empire*
when that curious news came through from Kittyhawk
and I think how disappointed I was
when I asked him what stood out
of all the change he'd seen
and he answered smartly,

> *People don't know the value of things anymore*
> *because nothing takes any effort*

realizing only now
how disappointed he must have been
with me

The Word

Making up my journal I write
that I was half an hour late,
realizing as I do that
I was really only fifteen minutes late
but leave it, thinking
what difference will it make
when I check next year?
But it's just that which bothers me,
the great finality with which
this tiny fact will be lost
if I leave the words stand.
It's like Norman Point.
For the first thirty years I lived here
Norman Point was all I ever heard it called
honouring a pioneer we all knew
but far-away bureaucrats saw fit
to change it on the charts to Daniel Point
after some low-level English naval officer
who paused here briefly long ago.
We locals scoffed and paid no attention
but pioneers disappear as tourists multiply,
and now Daniel Point is all I ever hear.
The printed word, allied with passing time,
sweeps all before.
The Word. It was not first, but it is last.
All its vaunted power is no more than this:
the Judeo-Christian way prevailed
because they wrote it down.

Dante's Wife

It was a good thing I guess
getting chucked out of Florence
if you care about writing.
He'd never have done the book
if he'd gone on at home, that's for sure.
Politics, politics, politics night and day —
that's all he ever did here.
They'd come to him in the wee hours
with some damn piece of scribbling
that couldn't wait for morning
and him the everlasting perfectionist,
every handbill had to go though twenty drafts.
I got after him — and who wouldn't —
we saw postings come and go
to men without a patch on him
he being too busy abetting zealots
to write a word in our own cause, too busy
offending those who could have helped him
for my sake if not his.
And he was a fool in politics.
He never grasped the simple brutality of power
for all his long-winded notions —
even I could see that.
Yet he couldn't leave it alone.
He promised, but his promises were as
those of an opium fiend. Finally
the fools talked themselves into real trouble —
he'd have been smoke if Rome hadn't spoken.
That was enough for me. Between that
and the sainted Beatrice with whom

no mortal woman could ever compare
the kids and I packed it in
left him suffer his banishment alone
even the Ghibbelines said I was hard
and maybe I was, leaving him wander
and ponder his folly
but that's what finally got him writing
if writing is what you care about.

City Poets

The city speaks greatly of its poets
with their own voice.
I am sick of city poets.
All they ever talk about is pus.
The void and pus.
The void is full of pus,
as the city floats on sewage
and nothing there is
in its skin; love,
for instance has the skin
of love, inflated
only with their lack of it.
Work likewise is
bothered out of its own self.
Life is.

                          In the country

poets speak of trees
and the price of fish
leaving life
to speak for itself.

bp nichol October 1, 1988

In the deluge of encomia
)there's a rare usage for ya beep — you like? no? oh.
anyway in the flood of inmemoriesof and specialissuesof
that will surely be turned loose by this
let me be first out of the gate
not that I was the first among praisegivers
to the living nichol
as a writer I thought he fooled around too much
and claimed too much for it
or allowed others to
and it's not as if he didn't get enough written
and as far as that goes if he wasn't so damn
promiscuous in his imaginings
the doctors might have found it harder
to persuade him that fifty-pound tumour on his ass
was in his head all these years
but I always heard he was a nice guy
and as his backcover photo aged and thickened
he came to look like a nice guy
and when I met him briefly
he seemed the nicest of nice guys
and then of course you always heard too
that he ran some sort of help centre for the fucked-up
and it's for that, a top Canadian poet
who was nice to the core and stayed that way
and who did something useful he didn't have to and kept
        at it
that I honour his contribution
as unique
and his loss as dear

Closeup

This poet I know
he's got a lot on the ball
I've seen him
rock auditoriums back
on their heels
and beard the biggest
bigwheels, but here he is
I know he's broke
and badly in debt
looking at this deal
I've tried to set up
that has to be signed by Monday
It will fix me up
for a whole year, he says
with what seems to be relief
but he's fixing his house
this week, adding a
room for the baby
and he misses the interview—

there is a logic
of immediacy
of closest things biggest
a transfixed stare sometimes
reality can't break in on

Undermined

Long past midnight
long past caring
whether I live or die
but still desperate
to make the printer's
deadline for this book
I struggle to rebuild in my
tattered fragment of mind
some sense of how this
heaving mass of verbiage
might strike the casual,
carefree first-time reader
only to realize after
reading the first line over
fourteen or more times
I have no idea what it says
finally just reading
letting the blur of type
run over my burning eyes
like a stream of clear
meaningless water
knowing when I'm finished
there will be something,
an infinitely distant trace
of feeling I can trust,
admitting,
when absolutely forced to it
it all comes down to
the undermind

Low Ebb

Words came to my lips for so long
like gifts from an unknown
benefactor, bright words live
with rhythm, more than their meaning,
that I am at a loss to look
for where they stopped.
I could see the main track always
well enough to run a smart counter
to it, now lost in fog, moving
at the mercy of whatever befalls.
I wonder if it was something
I inadvertently inhaled,
something deadly for packing parcels,
something fuming under the sink —
is a rare virus at this moment
blooming scarlet in my inner brain,
pressuring the very kernel
where psyche and flesh unite?
Or did the easy genius of youth depart
like a whiff as I passed my forty-fifth year?
If I was an Indian and had a soul
I could say it was lost
and hire somebody to find it —
all that is left to an aging WASP
is to stagger onward, puffing,
like when a strange noise develops
in the engine of your car
and all you can do is wait
for it to harmlessly go away
or declare itself in terms

catastrophic but clear.
It's just that I've never come up
from anything quite like this:
right when you think you've got used to it
life throws you a pitch
you've never seen before.

Cups Hanging from Cuphooks

on the shelf remind me of something else.
I know what I mean.
But I could no more say
than copy Botticelli
with a whitewash brush.
Still, if I ever
get even a feather,
a toenail, a scale,
of that shy, uncatalogued specie
slipping into the shadows
between the distant trees
everybody from
culvert dwellers to trillionaires
skinheads to Sufi dervishes
even my old English prof
would gape
to hear of it

which is how I come
to be found here
covered in spilled
words, pawing like
a baby who espies a
butterfly
pointing and mumbling

The Dog in the Mountain

I never get tired
of looking at Anvil Island.
It's not like an anvil
and yet you can see
why they named it that.
The peak is like the shorter horn
of an anvil
sticking up instead of out
as if someone had
melted an anvil down
and it collapsed in on itself.
Dog Mountain is different.
I have spent hours looking
and never found that damn dog yet.
Those old explorers must have
had a bit of poet in them —
sometimes in their names for things
its not the likeness that counts
so much as the way you must
tilt your mind to see it

The Paintings of E.J. Hughes I
Nanaimo Harbour

This might be the bluest painting ever made.
And such blue! The rippled waters of the harbour
a deep almost purple near shore
a brilliant turquoise in the middleground
bordered by the tan of the islands
with their dry mossy rocks
the waters of the strait beyond clayblue
and then in back the hills of the mainland so blue
rising to the dazzling snow.
"That's the blue one," people say
but it is really a picture of Hughes' favorite subject
two steamers of the CPR flag, the *Princess Victoria*
steaming toward the dock at an unlikely rate of speed
and the *Elaine* already there discharging
a gaily colored horde and belching black smoke.
Those who don't know water will be troubled
by the way the picture breaks sharply in the middle
between the dark chop inshore and the mirror calm
next to it, further out, for how
can the sea be rough and calm at the same time?
The mind balks, yet the eye recalls such sights.
Hughes was by this time trying to live within the law
as far as reality goes, but the rebel in him still loves
to seize a difficult truth and rub our noses in it.
The steamers are as brilliant in the sun
as gulls. Colorful as wood ducks.
Neither ever looked so fine, the ventilators
gaping vermilion, the *Victoria*'s lattice railings
like starched lace, gulls scattering astern
like confetti

"A beautiful ship," he says passionately
as if he could pay it no compliment fine enough
for relieving so gracefully
this relentless blue
he must paint for the rest of his days.

The Paintings of E.J. Hughes II
Christie Pass, Hurst Island 1962

I have never been to Christie Pass on Hurst Island
but I know the fishermen call it God's Pocket
so many have vanished in the great void of open ocean
between its small perfect shelter and Safety Cove
far across the Sound. Hughes knew nothing
except what his eyes had taken in
in a life of intense watching
but how he knew it! Stopping over at Christie Pass
only as long as it took to fill the small
last-chance fuel tanks with marked gas and stove oil
for the tiny, short-hopping gilnetters
and gyppo camp-boats with their one-lung Easthopes
he felt its precarious hope
though he came aboard a fat tanker
safe in the lap of the Rockerfeller empire
the rickety two-log floats clinging
awkwardly to the left of his canvas a
CPR steamer probably the *Norah* ploughing
briskly down the steamer path beyond
three trollers rafted together
and hung off the end of the wharf
to make room for his tanker which must
for lack of space, tie up only by the bow
dwarfing the miniature harbour
as two more fishboats approach, running for cover
in comradely tandem. A stout woman
in an apron leans over the two-by-four rail
at the base of the gangplank leading down
from the unseen camp, heaving a dish of peelings
into the water behind a clinker-built kicker

probably her own and over this whole scene of
frontier impermanence a craggy, weather-beaten snag
raises its bony finger like a malediction.
It is just a passing moment in the history
of a place its own occupants would not
expect you to have heard of, and yet Hughes
has given it epic weight, distilling its
haphazard existence into a parable
whose meaning, half a century past,
still preys upon the mind.

Dead Farms

All the dead farms in the woods
it was the Europeans who did it
they thought their world
their cups of tea their cricket scores
orchards operas oldcountry habits
meant something final
meant a world that went everywhere
and just existed
they did not know or forgot
a world is a fiction
which vanishes the minute
there is nobody to believe it
they forgot life was something else
something primal and terrible
rustling in the underbrush

Matilpi

On the beach at Matilpi
are the shells of over a billion clams
you can see them for miles
flashing in the sun
shaped by the shoreline
furrowed by waves
some shells whole
most broken shards
where
are the people who ate
a billion clams?

The glaring whiteness
undulled by fire-ash
tells us Matilpi
was always a place
to visit, to gather
not to live.

Below, the tide straining past
makes a taut sheet of the lagoon
wheeling galaxies of plankton by
feeding the great clams, the armies
of eating crab that clank
ponderously in their armour
along the lip of the rising tide

the beach runs up
to the cabin door
heavy with signs of ancient
and recent occupation

a bleached white bearskull
among the chin-high
artichoke and nettles —
a good crabtrap, a shovel
an axe, a light anchor
for fishing cod
lay in the open
like a challenge, untaken,
to intruders

and on the wall inside
a verse:
better to have never
seen the truth
than to know and not live it
some young Indian girls
camped here last summer,
from the city

and beyond the shells
a rock face, covered
with red ochre figures
some smeared
by the years it took
to eat and then forget
these clams
some with eyes still clear
staring
at the people passing now
who smirk at the notion

truth could be one simple thing
and pointing
say
I wonder what they mean?

Oolachon Grease

Oolachon grease gold, you hear about it
how the Tsimshian empire held
the whole coast to ransom for it
brought the poor Stick Indians begging
from the interior, beating paths
between the mountains you could
follow in the dark, by nose
the "grease trails" that let the
whiteman in, later on —
a beautiful woman professor told me about it
paler than butter she said,
but like butter without salt
and not at all repugnant to
the European palate
used as a condiment
but I ask you, are empires
sustained by condiments?
It was their oil, for the flame
in the flesh and more
I found it finally
in Bella Bella 1992 price $120/gal.
and it smelled like the cracks
between the deck planks of an old fish barge
if you can imagine spreading that
on your bread — quite enough to hurl
the European palate toward the nearest
toilet bowl which is how far
Indian is from White how far
learning is from knowing how
far we are from this ragged place

we've taken from them, for that,
the smell that comes of fish waste
thrown aside and let go bad,
that is the old smell of the coast,
known, as scent is the final intimacy
known of lifelong mates

take that barge plank, let it toss
ten years on the tide, knock on every rock
from Flattery to Yakutat, bake another
ten in the sun, take it rounded like
an Inuit ivory and grey as bone
crack it open and sniff the darker core
and you will know
what Vancouver knew ducking through
his first Nootka door pole, the essence
the odour of their living here
and however far you are from loving that
is how far you are
                    from arriving

Domanic Charlie's Last Forecast

All these nice people
business friends of the council
rich logger known for his
dealings with Indians
CBC producer known for
casting real Indians
in some supporting roles,
visiting chiefs,
the more presentable of the band —
wives of the young councilmen
dressed to the nines
and Jean Chretien

All assembled at the home of Chief Joe
after opening the new centre,
jammed together on a sofa
of impossibly rich silver brocade
the wall behind bare plasterboard
beside me sits this amazing creature —
an antique man like a breathing mummy
head like a snakeskin-covered skull
hands chimp-like and curled
around a yellow cedar eagle
carved on top of a cane
eyes like caves in a cracked rock face
long tunnels, dark, drawing back
to a distant place of light

Too astonished to be proper
I blurt, *Quite a show Hank puts on!*

snakehead rotates toward me with its
strange eyes
rock face breaks in a grin
A good show! it says
with a child's brightness
asks me what I do and six
minutes later proposes a book
this is Domanic Charlie
last great storyteller
of the Squamish people
famous on radio as
the old Indian weatherman

Well, Domanic! booms the big chief,
pumping the chimplike hand
What's yer weather pre-dickshun
for us this winter?

      Ten feet of snow!
      Ten feet for you, Hank Joe!

He spoke it like a joke
and we all took it like a joke
(the all-time record was about six)

By the time the clouds came that fall
old Domanic had gone to his last deer dance

but we got ten feet of snow
a good ten feet

The Raven

flimsy in wind
the raven pulses
the distance
flopping his way
down the valley
the instant our
engine noise ends

wings scraping air
drops on the tailings pile
loosening pebbles which
scatter down
toward our lunchbags

his blackness
a hook
in the eye
blinding noontime
coat quilted coal
of a charred stump
legs blackened wires
eyelids ash-blue
head
a hangman's hood

black at our backs
like a brush
of night at the heart
a rip in the
bright fabric of day
we fill with

sandwich bread
hoping he will
go away

seeing what Poe saw
what the Inuit
saw, even loggers
with dark thoughts of
dead friends come back
and no bird
not osprey condor
swan even eagle
held the Indian mind
like raven

in one myth a swan
white as cloud
burned for his vanity
surviving like this

I brought a camera later
thinking to have it
on film but
it came out
black

Be Careful How You Die

I have yet to see anybody who doesn't mess it up at the
     end.
The sainted old writer slowly dying all those years
so feeble and rotted in body
so gleaming and fine in spirit,
teasing us out of our too-easy gloom
infecting us with his case-hardened optimism
I thought he would be one
who could make the exit gracefully
and he got within a few months of it
then his saintliness turned sour
and he went out a cursing misanthrope
just like all the others.
I saw him within hours of his exit.
I came into his room when he was sleeping.
His back was to me, bare, and I was amazed
to find the skin of that sickly torso
a flawless creamy-white
but what I can't erase is the imprint
of his small pleated anus, yellow as a daisy
planted on his ancient bottom.
And old Joe—he was a guy if there ever was.
Logger in the old days, short-stake doryman,
boozer, founder of Simson-Maxwell,
lover and maker of history—he, too,
offered me a final view of his excretory pore.
This was after the last operation
when he got it re-routed through his belly.
He opened his pajamas just below the waist
and showed me this purple blob with Saran Wrap over it

like some bit of leftover seafood.
They call this the bud, he said.
Oh, Hi there, Bud, I said.
Yeah, meet my new friend Bud, he muttered,
indignant at the liberties
the doctors took with his body,
the obstacles everyone placed
in way of his simple wish to die.
It's all a bunch of crap he said
meaning everything we'd ever talked about
then totally out of the blue he added
The dames are all baring their arses.
The bathing suits are going to go up
so you'll see the cheeks of their arse.
How he, at 84, came upon this deathbed prophecy,
has troubled me ever since.
The next I heard he was under.
They were two big people in my life
men who shaped my way at crucial times
the one by saying *I did it and so can you*
the other by saying *don't be like me*
but when I think of them now
I can only see that yellow daisy
and that purple bud, and all I can hear is,
Their arses will all be hanging out. You'll see.
He was right. I do see, and every time I do
I think of old Joe. It is the easier memory of the two,
but I hope I can remember, when my time comes,
to lock myself away among strangers
who have nothing to lose.

The Time My Body Died

This one time my body died
so I put it in the freezer and froze it.
It bothered my family and friends
that I'd do that,
let my body die,
especially when I took it out
and stood it by the door
like a wooden Indian.
        "I don't like it," my wife said,
making no secret her suspicions
of my mental condition
        "You'll be sorry," my father said.
"The time will come you'll have to have it
and it won't be there."
I laughed off all their rebukes
and pretended I knew what I was doing
although I knew deep down
it was my own carelessness caused it
Still, I couldn't see what difference it made.
But people sure didn't like it.
They kept their own bodies alive,
even if they didn't know why
they went to a lot of trouble for it
and they really didn't like to see someone
make a mockery of their efforts.
I began to lose some of my bravado.
It was the body itself out there
on the front lawn
that seemed to start the trouble
standing there all grey and pasty-faced
confronting my neighbours

so I decided to brighten things up a little
by going out and putting some colour
on my face
with my kids' felt pencils.
It didn't work very well.
I ended up looking like a B&W photograph
touched up by a punker artist.
I began telling people I needed the body
for a scarecrow but they looked back at me
with a smouldering distrust.
Meanwhile the body was beginning to thaw
and my fingers were drooping like melted wax.
I decided I should probably dig a hole for the thing
but found myself reluctant to let go.
I'd had it such a long time
I'd become kind of attached to the thing.

Invisible Kid

When I was about five and we lived up the coast where
there was no radio in the daytime and TV hadn't
been invented
my mom used to read to me from A Child's Garden of
Verses.
She made it sound so sweet and nice like birds singing in
the trees or music on the radio and all the loveliest
things
but there was something funny about it, too.
Like when the man said When I was down beside the sea /
A wooden spade they gave to me.
In the picture it looked like the kid was digging with a
clam gun, but they called it the wrong thing.
And where it said The moon shines on the streets and fields
and harbour quays they had a picture of the moon
shining on a queer-looking wharf
like the one at Irvine's Landing except with the holes
between the pilings all filled up with boulders.
They called this a "quay" which rhymed with tree.
The book was full of wrong names for almost everything
but when I asked Mum it turned out they weren't
wrong, they were the names they used in the place
books came from, the big cities far away.
This made me feel very bad because I thought it must be
us who had the wrong names on everything.
My quilt wasn't really a quilt, but a "counterpane."
This happened each time we read books and it made me
think something wasn't right about the way we lived
in Green's Bay.
The things we did and the names we called them were
never the same as in books.

Dick and Jane never wore gumboots or lifejackets like me and my sisters did.

I began to feel the difficult world I shared with Mum and Dad and Uncle Charlie and the Poschners was somehow less than the world where books came from.

Recovering from that early conclusion has occupied most of the rest of my life.

The Good Woman

For fifty years at least work was all she knew.
She loved art at school but left it early
to look after her brother and sisters
tossing her girlhood away without a thought
dismissing her youthful beauty
for shut-away years in a farmhouse kitchen
then Dad took her away to more of the same
in gyppo cookhouses up the coast
doing the books at night
and raising us kids round the clock
but never a word of complaint did she utter
even when we broke her last piece of china
even when we got mad and misused her
she would hang her head and look away
waiting for better spirits better times
to come by. We all knew she was something—
she was wonderful and beautiful though
she always wore baggy old clothes
put aside her womanly beauty as she put aside her youth
she never cared about that, she just cared about us
she was always there when anybody
wanted a sandwich wanted a drink
wanted an answer or just plain love.
Dad had her wrestling with wrenches,
bleeding the brakes, spotting the truck—
she let her garden go to ruin for this
she was just there as selfless and changeless
as the spring rain or the southeast wind
she was there so long we forgot she was there
and then when we had gone long beyond

the time when we could think of her any way else
this selfless thing who just gave and gave
without any warning at all
she said enough of this
dyed her hair red
bought a car of her own that worked
moved upstairs to her own place
and took up art again
teaching me my greatest lesson about human nature:
you can never depend on it.

Oldtimer Abroad

You wouldn't have to climb a very high hill
to see all the places I've been he once said
which is why we bought him a ticket around the world
when he retired — not to be nice, not to make up
what we thought he might have missed
with his feet forever sticking out
from under some broken-down truck
black as a coal miner most of his days
putting his life on hold while he made a living
until one day he woke up old
we sent him for the sheer hell of it
to see what a west coast gyppo
would make of the Taj Mahal
He got out of his rickshaw to help
his skinny driver up all the hills
ended up eating with him on the little strip
of sidewalk that had been in the family for years
talked about the history of India and Margaret Trudeau —
"That man was every bit as good as you or me. In fact,
if I had a few like him in the old days
I could've made some money after all."
In Agra he fell in with another one
who slept outside his door, woke him at dawn
to see the Taj rise out of the dawn mist
found himself for the first time
in his long life weeping for sheer beauty
(hoped he wasn't going soft in the head)
In Bombay he slipped a fiver to a street beggar
touching off a spreading whirl of pandemonium
and would have been trampled as thousands rushed him,

had the police not appeared to beat them back with clubs.
In Nairobi bald-headed, beet-red, sweating like a pig
somehow he ended up living with a six-foot Masai princess
and never wanted to leave. Why he finally did
he never could explain. But when he got back
he was an unhappy man. He would stand at his window
looking out across the empty bush he'd spent his life
in thoughtless, happy contest with and say
"There's room out there for millions. It isn't right."
I worried then at the way we'd toyed with his identity
thinking we'd ruined one of nature's masterpieces
but his nature was of more resilient stuff than I imagined
and like a clearing in the rainforest
the memory was soon overgrown

Voices

The storekeeper was king in those years
and old T.T. Wade made the most of it —
my first clear memory of him
when I was about five
in town on the camp boat's grocery run
hanging around his general store after it closed
waiting for Dad to get out of Gordie Lyons'
he came out with the cash box
asked me what I was doing there
in this booming voice he always used
"Your Dad's in the pub again, is he?"
a fact I was trying to conceal
(how did he know these things)
I stammered that I wanted to buy some gum
"Gum," he boomed. "You wait here."
Unlocked the door again, came out
with a whole pack of juicy fruit
me digging out my change
"That's a gift from me to you" he boomed
in a voice so big I still feel small
Lord of all he surveyed in Pender Harbour

I still regard him as a Croesus
though the average cop earns more today
than he ever did back then
Later I worked there summers
crawling through the icehouse on my belly
wrestling slippery 300lb. iceblocks
wet sawdust going down my shirt
for 75 cents an hour

he had a list of ten things to do
whenever we thought we had nothing to do
wash windows sweep grounds straighten stock
you couldn't rest for a minute
you couldn't hide from him
and his big voice
we obeyed in little peeping voices
became adept at *looking* busy
while doing nothing
the hardest work I ever did
it was a habit that got me in trouble
the next year, working in the woods
for five times the wage
you were expected to go all out
when called upon, and the rest of the time
stay the hell out of the way
other guys would lean back and smoke
I'd be looking over my shoulder for ol' T.T.

He had my number from the start
to save space made me break up empty crates
before chucking them in the garbage bin
I would bash the slats to pieces
with my fists, enjoying the brutality of it
T.T. came up imitating Howard Cosell
"Here's Killer White landing a left, a right . . ."
his voice ringing off the rafters
got everybody to laugh at me
used a hatchet after that
feeling violated
in the privacy of my imagination

I could never hate him openly
for seizing the home of a sick worker
as if it were his sacred duty
or jeer at his English manner
like those who knew him only as
rich and ruthless
but had never felt the
icy reach of his mind

He grew old as I grew up
the town grew out of his grip
left him writing long letters to the editor
taking bows for those two-bit jobs he gave us
the eighties came and swung things around
I faced him across a council table
he stopped in the midst of a hot debate
to say his respect for me was at stake
but I saw him coming this time
shot right back, "Face it T.T.
you've never known respect
for anything but your chequebook!"
in a booming voice
he never returned to council
whispered I was dangerous
speaks to me now only when he can't avoid it
in a quiet voice

Klein Comes Back

Klein comes back years after
zig-zagging across the gym floor
of a dream in troubled times
Giddat ball! Giddat ball!
holding his pants up with
one hand, his glasses on
with the other, his voice full
of the elation that lured us
with childish delight
into our first chilling view
     of the mind's abyss

Lovely that schoolkid hush
about things like that —
it was not permitted
to say aloud the word *crazy*
within his hearing
and anyone who made fun of him
Gary Helmer would beat up.
The adults were his terror,
they and their unyielding realism,
old Freeman screaming,
holding up Klein's inksmeared paper
asking what sort of parents he had —
us at recess muttering, sure for once
of our indignation, *Freeman wouldn't
do that it he*
          knew . . .

And we were all so eager

to point to his hundreds in math
his strange flashes of knowledge
beyond us all, though usually
he never got his work started
head down in his scribbler
both hands full of snot
leaking down between his fingers
mixing with leaky ballpoint ink
muttering in strange voices
and giggling out of control

the teachers, those inadequate creatures,
always awkward, ignoring him
until drowned out by his
slurping noises —
Will someone please lend David a
hankie?
though no boy in town owned one

We returned to him in secret, following
him back to the lost kingdom of pretend
the adults pulled us away from
drawn irresistibly —
Where's the cancer bird, Dave . . .?
He said he was from another planet
and his tales of it, lasting hours,
still cause me wonder —

Once in gym class
teacher didn't like his wobbly pushups

ordered him up on stage
to do it properly
his prematurely hairy cock
fell out the rip in his jeans,
he pumped himself up and down
got it hard right there
in front of everybody,
giggling demonically
exploding the close fabric
they'd been weaving
around our minds

a furtive, guilty freedom
for which later
after they expelled him
and he'd blown our secret world away
in what they insisted on
calling a shooting accident
we dearly paid

A Fairly Honest Guy

I wasn't one of those little boys who
always tells the truth
I never told the truth
except by accident and
the only improvement
that came with growing up was
I learned how to lie more
realistically. Sometimes
I would find I was being so realistic
what I said would come true

and yet I think of myself
as an honest man

The Handkerchief Angle

I've sat down with some pretty fancy people now,
not royalty maybe but millionaires for sure
famous-in-Canada writers, members of parliament,
some regular staff members of the New Yorker,
the president of a major regional airline,
a well-remembered former NHL regular,
not quite the international jet-set
but plenty enough to make the cookhouse gang
back in Green's Bay feel smug about
predicting a great future for me
when I was five
but for all I seem to be able to get by
at these Manhattan coctail parties
I can't escape those cookhouse years
everybody must see it and I ponder
just what it is makes me different.

Today I think it might be handkerchiefs.
I don't use handkerchiefs. I have tried
but I don't have the habit
and it just seems too late in life to get it.
On the other hand I notice
almost everyone else I meet does, even
the revolutionary poet who refuses to use capitals
the oiler on the Queen of Coquitlam
and the homeless drifter thumbing a lift.
I trace my history back, searching
for the reason. How did I miss out?
Back in camp the men all blew their nose
by pinching one side closed
and giving 'er shit on the other side.

It works better than it sounds.
I can see them thoughtfully digging out
hard stuff with a black-nailed pinky
as they took instructions from the super.
When they got what they were after
they'd roll it into a little ball
and tweak it over their shoulder.
Inside if there wasn't a snoose can handy
it would get wiped on a thigh but only
in the politest company would you see it
dropped demurely into a shirt pocket.

This was my finishing school
and all considering I've survived it well
except for that one time at the Media Club
banquet in the Quarry House
where I forgot myself and pulled out a real
nugget while we were all sitting there waiting
to see if I beat out the editor of Vancouver Life
for first in the Prose Feature category
and went to tweak it under the table
but somehow it ended up
on the mayor's glasses

The Genius

In the city
I scavenge parking
spaces saving
my seven-fifty
— for being able to use
what others
miss or pass by
I credit my country
background, my
unregimented eye
it is the very keystone
of my self esteem
but my wife
sees it otherwise
always crawling
out the driver's side
shoefull of mud
other people
getting good sidewalk
— with you life is
always in through
the basement
fire escape
and you call it
an advantage

Small Blessings

People come to see us sometimes
we put them out in the back
Mare keeping them occupied
while I sneak out and hide
armfuls of papers in drawers
push things into piles
hoping they'll speak to us
in the morning — all that clutter
gotta trash it out some time
feeling especially guilty about this one
a well-known writer who deserves better
but he comes in says he was up
till 3 a.m. looking over our books.
Says his neck is still sore
from reading sideways.
What an amazing bunch of books
you have he says what a library
I just stick stuff out there
it's not a planned event,
I say. "It couldn't be," he says,
"It's remarkable."
I've never given a thought
to our books that way, what figure
we may have described
in our idle acquisitiveness.
I find myself basking in this
previously unsuspected
description of ourselves.
It was like the time in highschool
the principal said I stood

above all others for *poise*
something I had never aspired to
but seized upon with secret glee.
Sometimes you receive these little
unsought triumphs which are
no less delightful for
being worthless

The Made Bed

When we were first married and
lived in a pink trailer
we made love in the morning
with the opening day
the burst of birdsong
the sun fresh and damp like
a newly opened bud
     it was good to start the day
     in love
then came the kids
and our mornings were gone
our delicate and sustaining love
moved over
and another kind took its place
Silas slept in our bed
until he was three; Patrick,
whose appetite for warmth is greater,
was still there at five.

I stroke the curve of your morning hip
under the remoteness of the cloth
we never used to wear
and it seems to me the
miraculous innocence is still there
although our love has become
like an untended appletree
whose fruit are fewer and smaller
brilliant in their rarity
but less than the leafy abundance
that once was there.

This is a loss:
there is no avoiding it,
for all that the small shape
snuggled against your back
is a wonder our young lives
never knew. His desperate
affection cannot be denied
or resented
                    and yet our loss
can never, save in these
catch-as-catch-can moments
be recovered.

I suppose the reason
I have never tried to force
our own way is a neutral
satisfaction that life
doesn't always give
as it takes away.

Pinned Down by Love

You turned and soon
by the weight of your hip on my forearm
I could tell you were sleeping

First it just hurt
then it was tingling for awhile
now the arm is lost to all sensation

It will die, I think
Cell suffocation

It will be in the papers:
Man Loses Arm In Bed
and you will cease to love me

but I musn't wake you

Waves

She rises as
I fall
I try
to match my breath
to hers
which
though drawn in sleep
is shallower
and quicker

but the waves of her sleep
like those of the sea
have inscrutable
          rhythm

A Study

her flesh
clears

lights up
inside

by day
it is
opaque

her face
disfigured

with bus-
iness

now it is
water

before
a candle

it
is

the angel
again

First Poem of the New Space Age

In my livingroom this morning
they landed the first true spaceship
ushering in, as I think they said
a new era in space.
It was a nice day outside,
crisp and springlike, bright,
so my electromagnetic monitoring device
a twenty-inch Electrohome
its viewing screen slightly dysfunctioned
by dried fudgsicle but otherwise A plus plus,
was a bit hard to read and right on touchdown
I had to shift into repugnance mode
and go wipe little Silas' bum,
thinking what with the new era and all
it's probably time I repositioned my mindset
to accept the reality quotient of delayed replay
as equal to the original experience anyway.
A new era in space.
It's okay by me I guess, for all that I was secretly hoping
they'd fry themselves on the way back down
but that's just me.
I'm sure this space stuff is all good.
It gives them a way to burn off
excess productive capacity
without having to toast whole
cityfulls of third-worlders.
A new era in space.
This will stimulate the economy.
There will be a new spate of space
bestsellers, to be made into new space movies
setting us up for the real payoff:

new space-movie consumer goods.
What about that super-glue they used
to fix those pesky tiles on the heat shield?
I bet there's a sales campaign primed for release today
at hardware stores across the nation
"Glue that loose shower tile down with this
and meteorites won't move it, folks!"
We could use something like that around our tub.
No, space is good, even if it does
signal the final triumph of gimmicry over living
and make the young want to grow up to be robots.
It will allow mankind to re-stock one of its
most sorely depleted resources —
metaphor

Long Term Investment

Working on construction has cured me
of the old idea I started with
that damn near any sow's ear
of a clumsy, dumb, unwilling oaf
could be turned into a silk purse
of a journeyman worker
with enough canny planning
on my part and peer pressure
on the crew's, long since having
found you can do it twice as fast yourself
as try to train some dim-witted kid
who's going to quit as soon as you
get him to where he's any use to you
and chopping wood or refitting the boat
with my two young boys I find myself
grabbing away the hammer or brush
with the same practiced impatience
then stopping, thinking,
handing them back
beginning my rusty lecture on technique
knowing they won't get it this time
or the next time
or the next
but maybe the tenth time they will
and by the twentieth time
they'll be yelling at me
for being too old and slow —
it's hard to remember

anything long-term
is so rare these days

On the Evening News

"Roaring Sam" we called him,
a big frowning man full of ambition
who came in to clean up
after our tiny backwoods highschool
staged an infamous student strike
and was smart enough to see
the rebels had more than enough cause
in the grown-up delinquents on staff
succeeding by simply being normal
making Inspector for his pains
but he left a little scar on my ego
by once asking if there were any questions
about an upcoming field trip to Vancouver
to observe life in its civilized form
and when I put my hand up
hoping to impress the older kids
by asking the question they'd been musing
about all week, namely which
of our misfit teaching staff
might be going along to spoil the fun
replied in that dull roar he managed
for the most ordinary utterance:
"Are there any *other* questions?"
exposing me to a few deadly snickers
for which thirty-four years later
learning of his death
in a flaming bush plane
I must stifle a faint swell of triumph
the kind of thing that leaves no doubt
the soul of man came down
from a small, rat-like animal

Friends

We come to a time when
we just kind of say so what and not
care if we see them or not
and usually we end up kind of
falling together clunking
our beerglasses down not
saying much, you wonder
is this all there is, what
is this much-touted
human heart if it would
let one friend go take this other
friend's lifemate just out of
paltry appetite then laugh
as if their life was a joke
but the time comes
the fields of our lives'
orbits glow in a darkness
the injured one falls into arms
that know where to hold
we make our home yours
without thinking
get up at two in the morning
drive miles

Alter Ego Wanted

The one who isn't there, the one who isn't
there is the one I always want
that's the one could take you aside
say, hey, whatsa matter with you
you can't act like that
you're a lover not a fighter
you're a maker not a manager
you can't treat that woman of yours
that way, she's looking for love,
you're losing that kid of yours
what do you think you're doing
that's so important you can't
save your own flesh and blood
the one who could know enough
and have enough to grab your arm
and say wait a minute here
but I've moved away too fast
from all the ones who could have been
and nowhere in this blur of a world
is there anyone
          who gives a damn

After the Wake

Two lessons I have learned.
First, it's hard.
One doomed person
can outwit and out-work
a batallion of do-gooders.
Second, it's dangerous.
They end up hating worst
those who help them most.
I've never seen it fail.
And you are apt to hate them back
just as fervently,
your well-meant reasons
past recall.
The thing I really learned
is that
I am no hero.
It all too soon becomes
a question of
my own survival
and I always pick me
over them

You Tell Me

The kind of mess my yard is
I have no solution for
weeds rampant amongst good stuff
hedges of salmonberry and buttercup
overhanging the twisting
puny rows of spinach
affording a local base of operations
for the multitudinous vermin
that defeat me, but I will
not root them out, no:
I will not make demands
upon myself which in the end
might prove discouraging.
I know me. I must be
coddled along, if I am to
even keep up watering
through the season.
Low expectations are the key
to any dealings with me.
The house will never get painted.
The boat motor will never get fixed.
My book will never come out.
I have adjusted to these
realities, for nothing is so pathetic
as the slob with ulcers.
The thing that still gets me though,
is this neighbour I have.
He has a yard in which no weed
survives beyond the germinative stage.
It is like the miniature
Swiss town at Disneyland.

He also runs the waterboard
limits out in spring and coho
every Saturday, administers
a sprawling business empire,
has a wife and family who love him
and yet when I drop over
for some BS and coffee
he is always available
and to listen to us
there seems no essential
difference between us.

Fucking Slugs

All over outside you'll find them
in the first weeks of July
the black ones, not so much like severed penises
as the green ones, striated more like whales
small black landlocked whales
surrounded by portable, private
sticky oceans of slime
oozing their answer to everything
a scourge of such proportions even
the gentle Quaker Hubert Evans
was moved to muster Roberts Creekers
in an annual slug hunt that numbered
up to twenty thousand kills
and still never saved his leaf-lettuce
but if you watch them faithfully
some dewy morning you will see it
a couple sleek black bodies double-parked
they use that nostril-like pore
you may have noticed on the side
the black rolls back like a foreskin
out comes a white rig
so delicate and white
like white silk underwear
wavers out towards the other one
the eyestalks directing, craning
backward, everything so difficult
for slugs, so awkward, till
finally the two white things,
half the size of the slugs themselves
go into each other and relax
dissolving in a sluggish dream

of love on the damp leaves
you poke them with a stick
they go on dreaming
too lost in their dreams
to curl or unhook or ooze
and if the air is very still
and you cup your ear very near
you will hear a tiny disembodied noise
as if somewhere far across the valley
someone's record of Maria Callas arias
has become stuck on a high C
a gossamer thin musical shriek
which if you ever experience it
will leave you changed for life
so that no matter how much
leaf-lettuce you lose
you will never wish
to squish another slug

For the Birds

I want everything ordinary.
I don't want any big excitements
that might lead to trouble.
I forget how I got this way now
but I know I had my reasons.
I think it was all my friends
disappearing into black holes.
But it's tough, the way things are these days.
Dropping in on Pat and Lorna
for a few days, he sees the apocalypse
in every line, in every sip of wine
so I go with her to the store
thinking the brown grass and hard
clench of prairie fall might
spell relief but within a block
we're in trouble up to our necks.
A fat little bird of some prairie kind
is flopping around on a frozen field
having hit a wire and snapped its wing.
Instinctively I look away and keep walking
but no such luck: Lorna gasps, stops,
looks imploringly at me.
She is not used to walking with men
who shy away from challenges.
Her poems, too, are full of
daring words and scary revelations.
"Can't we do something?" she says.
"If Pat were here he'd step on its head," I say,
making no move to step on its head.
After an eternity of soul-searching
we walk away leaving the pathetic fluff-ball

reeling in the wintry dusk,
feeling morally squalid.

Years later I am in Vancouver
hurtling from door to door on business
desperate to get home that night
and I run up Werty's stairs hoping we can
get through his drawings in ten minutes —
right away I can see I'm in trouble:
Werty has this preoccupied look —
"We're in a bit of a crisis here," he says,
and it's the helpless bird thing again:
a baby robin has fallen down and crawled
into their yard just ahead of an army
of alley cats. Werty has put it up on the roof
but it can't fly and the parents don't show,
while cat eyes glint from every shadow.
I hope for a quick move by one of them,
but with the caution of the predator, they wait.
I decide to help search out the nest,
somewhere in the neighbouring yards
thinking only of getting Werty free for myself
but am mistaken for a back alley prowler
and end up fearing for my life.
I am too exasperated to be amused,
but Werty is in beyond my reach,
sensing the bird's peril like his own
me thinking maybe this is why he draws so well
so I call up the SPCA
but the tired voice just says the city

is crawling with fallen robins
and advises us to give it to our cat.
I end up driving Werty and bird to some sanctuary
far on the other side of the city
where it is assigned a case number
and we are advised on visiting hours.
"I hope you didn't mind," he says
and even though it's too late for anything
I actually feel sort of *good*
it was such a spunky little bird
when you got to know it

Which is the whole argument for the other way
what you get when you get involved
you get some nice little birds in your life
make connections with what counts
when I get back to where I'm staying
tell Bryan how I lost my day
he says, "Hey, I've got something to show you . . ."
hands me a new anthology of poems
"Haven't read it but I noticed your name here . . ."
It's a poem by long-lost Lorna
about that other bird

dedicated to me

Lull

My life runs along
like one of those little
runoff streams
charging down the slope
piling a dam of fir needles
in front of itself
stopping, backing
running off another way

right now the accumulation
of small tasks has me
stalled at my desk all
day, avoiding, giving in
to the promise of
a new project
but an hour into that
it has become another
blockage
and I catch myself
subversively wishing
for a
cleansing storm

Kinky

In half wakefulness you get a
glimpse of your life
passing through some trees.
It is important.
I get up in the night hoping
to see my life passing
over.

I used to get up at dawn
swim out to the island
sit naked on the rocks
watching the sun rise
hoping
to make myself different.
I hate not knowing
if it worked